# Sustenance for a Nourished Life

## A Beginner's Guide to Self-Mastery

### Rajani Lata

ISBN 979-8-218-13991-9

# DEDICATION

To all who have come before me and to all who will come after me. For those searching for meaning, seeking, questioning, yearning. I see you! I love you! Keep on questioning, keep on seeking within, because in you lies the spring that will nourish and sustain you into eternity.

To the woman I was in the past, and the woman I am becoming, every experience led me to you in this moment.

To my chosen earthly family for giving me the experiences that propelled me to my quest for meaning and purpose.

To my Papa for believing in me.

To Daniel, for holding space for my growth and enlightenment.

I am because of all of you.

Be well and Flourish,

Rajani

*"How you do little things is
how you do big things"*

Rajani Lata

# ACKNOWLEDGMENTS

I want to thank the universal consciousness for continued messages of encouragement and many times for literal words to flow through my hand as I complied those words and my thoughts since I began my search for meaning and purpose around 2007. Thank you for your guidance, silent nudges, and messages from what I can only call "messages from the universe" for the healing of human beings and for helping them become the best version of themselves.

This book took 15 years in making as I went through my own journey of self-discovery and human experiences, so I want to thank all those that touched my life and taught me lessons on self-love, forgiveness, and inner wisdom. While it took 15 years to compile, the book itself is my own life experience dancing with the universe, opening up to its mystical encounters, and in essence learning to create my own reality from within. Thank you to those who have touched my life in various ways.

I also want to thank all the physical and non-physical bookstores for making my book available to anyone with a desire for self-mastery to manifest their own journey of self-discovery, purpose, and service to humanity.

For now, and forever.

# TABLE OF CONTENTS

# PREFACE

I welcome you to this book of self-mastery as a path to self-discovery, happiness, and your connection to humanity and universal consciousness.

This book is a result of my own life experiences and quest for a higher purpose, resulting in me seeking growth through education, self-help, and questioning who I am. I was never satisfied with the superficial and had an inner knowing that life was more than being born, eating, sleeping, and doing as I was told.

The urge to compile my experiences and thoughts into a book started happening in my second year as a doctoral student as I started devoting more and more time to the discipline of self-leadership. I have been fascinated with how I can become the best version of myself and what my purpose is on earth. Those two questions kept on surfacing as I tried to find my place in the corporate world, training adults in a healthcare setting. I discovered that I was more interested in their well-being over teaching them how to be competent at their jobs. I also found that if they were focused on becoming better versions of themselves, their performance was better as a result. During this time,

I started my doctorate in educational leadership, but I found that I was more focused on self-leadership classes– the more an individual is focused on their own betterment, the better leader they will be– which led me to publish my paper *The Development of Leaders: Being, Knowing, and Doing – Leading Through Self Mastery*.

After ten years in healthcare, I decided to quit due to a lack of growth and a feeling of disconnection. I then embarked on a journey of the way I envision leaders, leadership, and work of service to be. I listened to my inner calling for spirituality and healing arts and decided to devote my time to spiritual entrepreneurship through House of Rajani, devoting my time to coaching and mentoring adults who are seeking growth and life as they had learned was not working for them. During this time, I also started training in Usui Reiki and became an intuitive Reiki Practitioner. My quest for growth also led me on the shamanic path to deepen my knowledge and understanding of the universe and my place in it.

## Reading This Book

While you can read this book front to back, there is no right way to approach it. Each chapter can stand alone as a topic to delve into. There may be a reference to a word or sentence in a previous chapter, but each of the topics can stand alone. I recommend that you use this book in whatever way you feel called to and utilize the learnings in there. Use your intuition and let it guide you. Be playful and trust that you will be led to the right way to utilize this book for your own self-mastery.

This book is interactive and has space in several sections to write notes, deep dive into your inner consciousness, and co-create your own lessons. I invite you to make this book a part of your journaling and growth. Write, scribble, earmark, whatever it takes to bring out the best in yourself.

You have my permission to let go of what you know about how to handle a book and make it your own.

---

# Chapter One

# Message from the Universe

Let us talk about the vast expansiveness of the universe. The energy that trans-mutates through particles of light that then penetrate like a light beam into every living and nonliving element on this planet.

Unlike nonliving elements, living beings receive nourishment through these light beams in the form of sunlight, nature, water, air, food, and energy. To understand this, let me give you an example: food is made of the energy that grows with light provided by water, earth, sunlight; this provides humans energy. Let us think of someone in love. Although they forget to eat, they still feel complete. In these instances, this is because they feed off of the energy of that light, which is in our world, surrounding and encompassing us during our entire stay on this planet.

## *Human beings are capable of incredible feats.*

That light energy is the same and stays in and around us from the time of our conception to the time our soul leaves the body. The rise and fall of this energy that we experience are due to our mental perceptions and the limitations we create for ourselves in our hearts. Think of a thermometer that stays outside through the hot, warm, cool, and cold temperatures. You will notice the rise and fall of the mercury depending on the weather. Similarly, our internal temperature determines the ebb and flow of that light beam of energy within us.

## *The mysteries of the universe are meant to be felt first to be then seen.*

Human beings are capable of incredible feats, but we are limited by the degree of our connectedness to that light energy. The energy of the universe continuously flows, but our attachment to the beliefs that we have accepted as the reality or, in other words, our perceived truth about our surroundings prevent us from manifesting miracles that our light energy is capable of. Because they are unseen by our naked eyes, the hidden mysteries and powers are disregarded as myths, fascination's, illusions, and stories.

Nevertheless, why still the heart feels what the eyes cannot see? The mysteries of the universe are meant to be felt first to be then seen. Because in believing is seeing. If I gave you a piece of gold and you did not know its value, worth, rarity, or its significance, then to you, it is just a piece of shiny rock. Perhaps aesthetically pleasing for the eyes but still a piece of stone. To know its worth, you have to understand what it means to you.

Gold may not be a good example. Think instead of someone you love so dearly in this world; someone you will give your plate of food to and yourself remain hungry just so that they are not hungry in your presence. You know that person's value and worth to you are not the same by someone else's standards because you have given them a sacred space in your heart. Your feelings give importance to that person for you, not the norms of the society you live in.

*Feel your way around the universe, and the mysteries will be revealed to you.*

Do you get the idea?

In feeling, you find the value of someone or something, not the other way around.

Feel your way around the universe, and the mysteries will be revealed to you. So, in feeling is your true sense of identity.

## *Affirmation*

**Life is beautiful, succulent,
luscious, and decadent. I want to
taste every morsel of its tantalizing
offerings. I want to bathe in its
sacredness, quenching pure delight,
and indulge in the life of my dreams.**

In spite of the tremendous pressure from society to be a certain person or certain self, it is vital for you to remain in your power. When you let others dictate your every little move, you lose your rhythm and essence because your all-knowing self does not feel heard, and suppression leads to a place of complacency and numbness. However, do not assume that nothing is happening at this level of feeling or state of being.

This is very important so pay extra attention! It may look as if nothing is happening on a superficial level, but on a micro level in your body, your cells are acting out. It sometimes takes months or years to see the effect of not listening to your body. It takes pressure to force your intuition and body to become disconnected and conditioned to follow the dictation of words coming outside of the self. For example, others like families, teachers, bosses, or anyone who you have willingly or unwillingly decided to defer to and mold the self into what everyone else prefers. Your body revolts! Typically, that revolution comes in the form of illness, suffering, pain, and loss.

Honor yourself. Trust your intuition. Be the shero or hero of your own life instead of playing a supporting role in someone else's drama. When a situation or person does not feel right, be okay to let go.

## Exercise

How do you honor yourself?

_______________________________________________

_______________________________________________

_______________________________________________

_______________________________________________

Remember, honoring yourself must feel right to you. You should create ways that you feel peace in actions that show you respect your inner moral compass. Let go of past failures and ways you let yourself down. Be in the here, now and sit up.

Honoring yourself can look like:

- Taking a shower and wearing clothes that make you feel good even if you are not going out of the house.

- Consuming the highest quality of natural food you can afford.

- Sitting down and consuming your favorite beverage without distractions of social media, work emails, etc. in a meditative way.

- Being thoughtful in your actions, words, choices.

- Slowing down, and focusing on one task, giving it your full attention.

- Consuming media that supports your well being instead of those that increase your anxiety.

## Personalize an affirmation to honor yourself

I honor myself by ______________________________
because it ____________________ me ____________________.

Example: I honor myself by <u>juicing everyday day</u> because it <u>gives</u> me <u>a sense of health and powers my day</u>.

Example: I honor myself by <u>meditating</u> because it <u>allows</u> me <u>to be mindful of my thoughts</u>.

## Balance is Key

Balance is Key

# Chapter Two

# Moving from Fear to Freedom

Fear is crippling. It comes in many different forms. Fear is a feeling that attacks our sensibility and makes us weak and vulnerable. It can also make some individuals aggressive, distrustful, and mean to others who, they feel, are attacking their sense of safety or security. Fear is an absence of love for self. It is a feeling of not measuring up in others' eyes when instead the perception of measuring up is really one of our own insecurities.

*Fear is an absence of love for self.*

Fear grips our senses, rattles our sensibility, and stops us from seeing things rationally. When we are fearful, others can instinctually feel that, and in worst-case scenarios use that to bully, abuse, and harass us. So let us not give anyone that much power over us. What should you do when faced with something you fear?

## *The sense of fear is greater than the fear itself.*

First of all, it is essential to acknowledge that you are feeling the fear. Be it fear of public speaking, fear of a bullying coworker, fear of the health challenges; for the most part, the feeling of fear is in your head. The sense of fear is greater than the fear itself. Admit that you are fearful of the situation, person, incident, and then find the courage to love yourself despite that feeling. I know this is hard.

Breathe in and out slowly and tell yourself that "I love me" or look in the mirror and say "I love you." Acknowledge your feelings and let the feeling of love wash over your body. Say positive affirmations such as:

- I am strong
- I am courageous
- I am sincere
- I am a good person
- I have a good character
- I am good at ___________________

- I am_________________________________
- I am  _______________________________
- I have  ______________________________

When faced with fear, instead of taking the fight or flight stance, take a few deep breaths and say in your mind, "I can do this;" " I am bigger than my problem." Fear is nothing but your body sending you alerts to change the course of your life. It is like an alarm to warn you to pay attention to your environment or your situation, and it is showing you signs and warning you that you are not in sync with your environment or your environment is not in sync with who you are meant to be. Fear is alerting you to change your mindset, behavior, thought, and/or your circumstance.

When you see yourself as your fear, you should take a pause and breathe. Notice how I have said to breathe so many times. Because breathing is an action that first and foremost shows you that you are alive, and pausing to breathe allows you to think rationally about your perceived danger.

In America today, millions of people are taking prescription drugs for anxiety and panic attacks and have not done a thorough investigation inward to find the root cause of their symptoms. When you look at fear head-on and admit the root cause of that fear, you are in a far better position to find a solution. Sometimes fear is elusive, and there may be no visible explanation of its source. For instance, a negative self-image can turn into a fear of judgment from others. That negative self-image, along with the fear, can ride with us during our entire lifetime. When we can admit and acknowledge all fears, we can deconstruct those feelings and allow them to dissipate instead of catching a ride on our life journey. Another example could be that your parents did not give you the attention you needed growing up. As an adult, you may have a fear of trusting others, which can interfere in forming friendships or relationships.

Now take a moment to work through your own fears in these exercises.

### Exercise

What are you fearful of?

_______________________________________________

_______________________________________________

_______________________________________________

_______________________________________________

Why are you fearful?

_______________________________________________

_______________________________________________

_______________________________________________

_______________________________________________

What can you do today to get rid of the fear and embrace the situation with love?

_______________________________________________

_______________________________________________

---

What would your world look like if you did not have this fear?

---

---

---

---

Now, create your world in the way that you re-imagined even while the fear is there, and let it dissipate as you live the life you imagined.

### *Affirmation*

*Fear is the absence of love. I love
my life. I love myself. My fears shine
a light on my hidden pain. I gently
embrace my pain and heal them with
love by taking care of myself. I listen
to my body. I listen to my heart. I
listen to my intuition. When I feel
fear, I ask my body what it needs, and
I listen to the response.*

# Chapter Three

# Surrender

For surrendering to the flow of the great universe is to be in sync with what is coming. No amount of fret, anxiety, fear, and pessimism will make things go faster than what is the universal law for your specific timeline of events. You must keep on walking in the direction of your desires and let the great universe do the rest. Think of it this way: in the animal kingdom, a human and nonhuman mother carries a fetus until it is time to deliver. Poking and prodding will not speed up the gestation period. It might hinder the progress instead. The baby may be impacted negatively if we poke and prod for the baby to appear quicker than what is naturally appropriate.

Similarly, planting a seed and checking it daily for germination and fruition will not give you the fruit by any natural means. There are stories of expediting the fruit-bearing process, but the result may not be to your liking. We all have tasted strawberries ripened naturally and those that ripened in the warehouse. Do you get the idea?

---

## *You must keep on walking in the direction of your desires and let the great universe do the rest.*

---

Slow down, and tune into your timeline. Your timeline is as different as the lines on your palms. Your timeline is precisely that, just yours. So please do not compare your success or lack of it to others around you. If someone compares you to others, do not take it personally. Not taking their comments or comparisons personally requires you to be fully aware of your strengths and weaknesses and full awareness of being enough wherever you are on your journey.

Do not engage in self-doubt or argue with someone who tells you how you need to be. Your self-growth is yours– you can help or hinder your growth. However, it does not impact how others will see you. Others will view you in their image and measure your worth based on their own self-worth. If you use others to measure yourself, you will always be disappointed. This is not the way to live. Your worth is beyond measure because of the fact that you are on this earth. You are complete. Being here is your birthright.

It is your job to unravel all the traumas, conditioning, societal pressures, and limitations put on you since you were born to now— to the moment that you came into your self-awareness. From here, your only responsibility is to unravel the knots that cause you anxiety, pain, and fear. Then you breathe healing love in those areas of your body and mind so that you can allow the process of divine energy to move through you without any blockages.

Energy cannot move through stagnant areas. Think of a rock in a stagnant pool of water. The rock is just sitting there, and the water moves around it, not through it. The same is with energy in the body. Think of traumas, no matter what size, like rocks; trauma can be big, small, or medium, and they all create blockages.

## *Your timeline is as different as the lines on your palms.*

Someone broke your heart, your father left when you were a toddler, you did not get accepted into the college of your dreams, or someone abused you for years. All these bottled-up pains are like coal under pressure, but instead of turning to diamond— which is still a rock, pain in your body, specifically in areas like your heart, stomach, chest, etcetera, create blockages. So while energy still flows, it is not able to move freely. Like water moving around the rock, the energy in your body also curves around those blockages. Resulting in a lot of hard work, but the results may not be something you are happy with.

---

## *Energy cannot move through stagnant areas.*

---

Have you ever asked yourself, "What am I doing wrong?" or " I am doing all this work, but why am I not seeing any results ?" Do not be disappointed! Keep on doing the work. There is no other option. For if you stop doing the work, the pain will remain, and it will take another shape, but it will continue to create barriers to your self-growth and enlightened state of life. For example, think of it as you do the hard work of connecting to an estranged parent or friend, and upon receiving no validation from that person, you stop reaching out and think, "why bother." If by stopping to reach out, you also eliminate the inner healing work, then you will manifest hurt and pain in other relationships of yours. So while it is not essential to physically tell a person who hurt you how much hurt they caused you, it is most crucial to reach out metaphysically and etherically. For only your healing is your responsibility. Once you heal a specific area of your life, then and only then can you help others in that same journey. Self-healing is a lifelong process. Therefore each individual is responsible for one's own healing.

In the stages of healing the self, awareness is the first step. You probably have heard of the saying, " if you can name it, you can deal with it." I suggest you go a step further and say, "If I can name it, I can heal it." Once you are aware of the way pain, fear, and trauma manifests in your body, start asking the question, "What is my lesson in this?" "What is this pain wanting me to learn about myself?" "What am I called to learn from this?"

Remember, emotional pain is caused by not one event. Emotional pain is a continuous pressure that causes trauma. Dealing with emotional pain requires a level of trust in the universe. Keep in mind that the universe has your back! Earlier I said, " you are enough, and that is your birthright." Trust that!

## *Self-healing is a lifelong process.*

It is also essential to do the healing work so you can move through all the pain and transform. How you got the pain is not your fault. Perhaps you trusted someone innocently, and they betrayed your trust; maybe you were a child and could not defend yourself or your loved ones. But healing yourself is your responsibility.

Hurt people, hurt people! (Think of what this means for you?)

Without healing, we continue to engage in generational pain. We continue to engage in traumatizing others like we were traumatized. We violate others like we were violated, and the cycle continues. So instead, surrender to the great universe and allow it to work through you for healing.

Earlier in the chapter, I talked about the rock in stagnant water and how the rock sits in the middle of the still water. Now think of a rock sitting in flowing water, slowly, day by day, the water chips away at the big rock and makes its way through it until one day POOF!, the rock is gone. Disappeared. On day one, looking at the rock, you may not be clear how it will disappear, but it does so in due time. Similarly, the healing work of unraveling your emotional pain requires slow and steady, continuous work. Think of a very knotted ball of yarn. If you pull fast, you will create more knots. Slow, meticulous pulls take time, but if you are diligent, then you have a somewhat wrinkled but workable ball of yarn to make into whatever you like. The same applies to your emotional healing work.

## Exercise

Work through your pain, asking the questions that come up. There is no right or wrong question. The only important thing is to ask and, if possible, write down the questions and answers. I have made sure to put note lines so you can engage in this activity if you choose. Ask the questions genuinely, without judgments, and look for signs and messages. Remember that the great universe is excellent at giving messages in every way possible. Everyone or everything can become a Messenger if you are tuned in to receive divine messages.

## Story Time

### *Reach*

*I will tell you a story about receiving a divine message. It happened to me on one fine evening.*

*It was a day like any other in 2015. I came home from work, and I was going through some dark times in my personal life. I was caught in my own despair over desires and wishes unfulfilled. It occurred to me to ask the great universe to give me a sign if I was on the right path. I asked the divine to show me that it was listening to me and that it was there for me.*

*I kept on saying, "Just send me a message," "Any message," "Show me a sign," I begged. Finally, I went into the bathroom to brush my teeth. As I was brushing my teeth, my eyes looked down at the teeth floss package with a brand name "Reach." I said to myself, "Haha, very funny." "I don't believe that is a sign. To the universe, I said, "That teeth floss was already there; you didn't try hard enough," "Do you really want me to take this as a message?"*

*I thought nothing of it, and I went to sleep. The next day I went to work, and my colleague and I were talking about ourselves and self-help and healing, and I told her about the incident the night before, and how I said that was so easy, I don't know if I can trust it. My colleague said, "Hey, wait a minute," as she fumbled through her pockets and then went digging in her purse.*

*She pulled out a rock that she carried with her, and on the rock was carved the word "REACH." I was blown away. I asked for a sign, and as I was still not believing what I saw on the teeth floss package, the universe showed me the words carved on a piece of a small rock. Yes, I am a believer that if you are willing to listen, anything and everything is a message from the divine universe. You just have to ask for it. And if you are a slow learner, then the same message will keep appearing until you pay attention and seek to interpret the message.*

*So, you see, the universe is responding. Are you listening?*

*Remember to play like your life depends on it. Because it does!*

# Sacredness

The word sacred, to many people, is a word loaded with fear of wrongdoing and punishment. Why? Because many associate this word with the opposite of religion or non-sacredness because of how our culture has indoctrinated values and morality in the fabric of our society. Think of sacred as a way of being that always is with you as a person moving through your life choices.

Sacredness is how the divine energy of the great universe moves and flows through you by the way you walk, talk, interact, respond, engage, and most importantly, how you carry your Self at a moment in time. How you are present in any given moment is sacredness. If you are in fear, no matter how great a place you are at, you will not reap any benefit of the moment because of the way your body reacts to the presence of fear, which can manifest as pain, anxiety, or detachment. This is the same reason that many people who have been abused block out days or years of their lives. Because the fear and pain are overwhelming. What happens then is those blocked-out pain "rocks" stay in the body and continue to create blockages.

## *Sacredness is how you see yourself in your worldview.*

If you yourself or anyone else you know is going through this type of detachment, give love energy to those traumatic times, and be present as a willing listener to the needs of the body or the individual. Sometimes being present is all it takes to be seen and accepted. Sacredness is how you see yourself in your worldview. Following doctrines while judging a homeless person lying on the side of the street is not that. We all are guilty of moments of thoughts where we judge someone. How we judge others is a direct measure of how we judge ourselves. Read that again!

Think of it as garbage in and garbage out or love in and love out. What thoughts are in your mind where no one can see or read you? Purity of thought is in compassion, kindness, humility, and love. If you give all of this to yourself, there is no way, and I mean no way anything else will be in your heart for others. So align yourself with the divine and practice sacredness as a way of being. The rest will shape up from there.

The most important thing is doing the self-work. How you treat others and how others treat you is just a reflection of how you treat yourself. So please treat yourself with love and flow through your life with the awareness that you and others are divinely connected in this great universe.

*Purity of thought is in compassion, kindness, humility, and love.*

## Exercise

List examples of times when you judged others:

___________________________________________________

___________________________________________________

___________________________________________________

___________________________________________________

What was your state of mind when you were judging others?

___________________________________________________

___________________________________________________

___________________________________________________

___________________________________________________

Knowing what you know now, how will you transform those interactions by honoring the sacred in you that is reflected in how you see others?

___________________________________________________

___________________________________________________

___________________________________________________

___________________________________________________

# Chapter Five

# Mindfulness

Mindfulness is an awareness of ourselves and our surroundings. I would like to bring this topic from the mundane, thrown into the conversation casually, to actually breaking it down to its granular level and discussing why mindfulness is such an important subject. It is the right time to discuss mindfulness in the world today because we are on the cusp of breakdown as a society. We need individuals to understand and practice this reality and then apply it to their families and communities' microcosm to move forward as a wholesome society.

Why is mindfulness like an endangered species today? In society today, we exist separately yet together. We need to instead function together, yet individually.

What does this mean?

Think of a bus full of people as a small society. The individuals are separate, doing their own separate things, functioning separately, some chatting, many on their phones, with earbuds in, bumping into each other, apologizing or not, all on a crowded bus together. This is how we are as a society. This is an "I and my" society instead of an "us and we" society. We want to be first in line, first to get a chance or an opportunity, and first to succeed. To make your individual dreams come true, you will trample over others who are around you. Again, think of the bus scenario. You have somewhere to go, and you will compete with all others around you to get in early so you can get a seat and you can reach your destination. This happens everywhere. I am not saying everyone is like this, but we are acting like this as a society.

---

## *You are the one who gives others permission to treat you in one way or another.*

---

Mindfulness is a practice that allows us to stay in our power with a firm belief that if it is in my destiny, then I trust in the universe I'm going to... (insert whatever it is ). With mindfulness practice, the journey is more important than destiny. The practice of mindfulness requires us to pay attention to every aspect of our actions and events of the day.

Challenging, is it not? It is easier to stare into the space aimlessly and blame others for doing to us what we have been doing to ourselves: ignoring certain aspects of ourselves, which in turn has a chain reaction in how others treat us– just the same way we treat ourselves. Remember that you are the one who gives others permission to treat you in one way or another. It is this simple.

## *When you are mindful, you are aware of what is going on in your body.*

Mindfulness requires work. You have to know all parts of yourself to recognize any feelings of discomfort, uneasiness, pleasure, euphoria, and the like. When you are mindful, you are aware– constantly aware, of what is going on in your body. You can intuitively sense the level of comfort or discomfort with every step of your day. When you sense discomfort, it gives you a chance to talk to your body. First, ask your body what it is feeling? Where is your body feeling the discomfort, and then going through the most challenging part of that asking: why is your body feeling discomfort?

You can do the same for feelings of comfort, but humans are so busy enjoying the feeling of comfort and euphoria that who has time to ask questions? Intuitively, we know that our body is in tune with our feelings when we are comfortable, and our hearts and minds feel pleasure. But, on the other hand, discomfort is a disconnection of body, mind, and spirit, requiring more in-depth exploration.

Let's get back to asking the body what it is feeling.

Just like you would ask a child over and over again what it wants to eat or drink, in a similar way, when asking questions to the body, you have to be gentle. When we are in discomfort, like a little child, our body feels that it is not being heard, so it throws a tantrum. This tantrum can be in the form of illness, pain in the neck or shoulders, anger, addiction of any kind, or just a gut feeling.

### Mindfulness is an awareness of ourselves and our surroundings.

When you gently ask, you are letting the body know that it is okay to be honest. Like a little child who wants to tell the truth, but if it knows that telling the truth will lead to the caregiver's anger, punishment, beating, grounding, etcetera, the child starts making up stories. Our bodies and our minds can do the same, and for adults, lying can be seen as a mental health problem.

You have to tell your body that it is okay to tell what the discomfort or the problem is and that you will address it no matter how difficult it is for you. Because if you do not, then ultimately, you will suffer. Alone! But others around you, mainly your loved ones, will suffer secondary pain too.

Look around in our society; mental illness, addiction, lies, anger, jealousy, and other extreme pain are widespread.  It needs to stop. Mindfulness practice allows human beings to look within for healing instead of outside of the self. When practiced with utmost reverence, mindfulness will enable us to show compassion to our wounded parts and heal them before they become a problem.

Being mindful of ourselves and others means being aware, compassionate, empathic, kind, and honest to ourselves. Do not ever think that no one will know how you really feel if you keep things bottled up inside. All human beings have an inner knowing. Some more than others, but we all have little invisible antennas or radars. Just like when one yawns, another one in the vicinity will yawn as well. Similar to that, when one is feeling something, another can sense that something is going on.

---

## *Mindfulness practice allows human beings to look within for healing.*

---

Humans may not be able to know precisely what is going on, but we certainly feel when something is off. Have you ever felt a gut feeling or intuition about a situation or person you know you should not get involved in or with? And then you still went with your logical mind, which said there was no basis for your feeling because there was no evidence?

## Exercise

Write down some examples of when you went against your gut feeling:

________________________________________

________________________________________

________________________________________

________________________________________

How did you feel later when you found out that your gut feeling around that circumstance(s) was actually correct?

________________________________________

________________________________________

________________________________________

________________________________________

When you pause and do a check-in with your body, you will notice that after acknowledging the discomfort and the specific details about why there is a discomfort, soon after, the pressure of the discomfort will dissipate. Only long enough for you to take steps to rectify the situation. Suppose, upon listening to your body you take no action to honor the body's feelings and continue moving forward in the direction of pain. In that case, that pain eventually becomes chronic and takes on the form or shape of a disease.

All of us are currently dealing with some pain that we did not acknowledge and clear from our lives. It is now the time to work on cleaning this mess. Mindfulness begins with the self. You can begin the exercise of mindfulness by first deciding that you honor and respect yourself enough to trust and listen to your senses and intuition. When you decide that you will listen to your body, you are, in fact honoring the traditions of the ancient cultures where the sun, moon, earth, and nature were guiding humans throughout their days. When it was dark, it was time to sleep. When it was light, one woke up and took on the day. When hungry, then eat and when thirsty, then take a drink.

*When you are mindful, your internal compass will guide you.*

There was a balance, nothing was done in excess. Humans took what was needed and used them without waste. When you are mindful, your internal compass will guide you. You will recognize the value in doing the right thing because hurting or causing pain to self or someone will cause you distress. You will understand the importance of moderation because excess means you are taking someone else's share.

If you look around today, we are a society of excess; excess food, clothes, etcetera. We have this false idea that having excess will give us a feeling of grandeur. So we surround ourselves with things that take the place of people. In an "I" society, things provide a sense of accomplishment for a little while until we find another material or position to pursue. So we continue this pursuit and never actually arrive at a place of satisfaction. The joy that you get from helping another human being rise up from the shadows of their miseries or pain gives us far more satisfaction than what material things can do for us.

---

### *Mindfulness allows us to look with the inner knowing what the eyes cannot see.*

---

Do you know that in helping others rise is our fulfillment? There is never a greater satisfaction than in seeing someone grow with our help. Yet how often are we doing this? Just because we do not see the benefit doesn't mean it is not there. Mindfulness allows us to look with the inner knowing what the eyes cannot see.

Remember, that as a society, we need to function together with our own unique abilities and serve for the good of humanity.

## Exercise

What was your childhood dream of the work you wanted to do when you grew up?

____________________________________________________

____________________________________________________

____________________________________________________

____________________________________________________

Where did you see yourself living?

____________________________________________________

____________________________________________________

____________________________________________________

When did you change your mind about your childhood career dreams?

____________________________________________________

____________________________________________________

____________________________________________________

____________________________________________________

Why did that dream come to an end?

______________________________________________

______________________________________________

______________________________________________

______________________________________________

What is stopping you from working in the direction of your dream life?

______________________________________________

______________________________________________

______________________________________________

______________________________________________

What ONE thing can you do today in the direction of living a fulfilled life?

______________________________________________

______________________________________________

______________________________________________

______________________________________________

Who can you lean on for non-material support to inch closer to your fulfilled life?

_______________________________________________

_______________________________________________

_______________________________________________

_______________________________________________

If today was your last day on this earth plane, what are the FIVE most essential things you must do? And what is your message to others?

_______________________________________________

_______________________________________________

_______________________________________________

_______________________________________________

What do you know for sure?

_______________________________________________

_______________________________________________

_______________________________________________

_______________________________________________

@house_of_rajani
Breathe

# Chapter Six

# Destiny

Let us talk about destiny. Human beings have this idea that destiny is a path that life will lead to no matter what route you take in life. Instead, they forget that destiny is a collection of choices, decisions, commitments, and submissions you make throughout your life. It is not easier to blame life's results on destiny than to make bold choices that impact your quality of life. Usually, the word destiny or fate is brought up in conversations where someone has failed at something. Please do not give up and blame it on destiny; recognize that you have the power of free will.

Remember, destiny can be good as well. You can shape your destiny by your faith in yourself. You are the only one who knows how much mental, emotional, and other investments you have made in your dreams or goals. When your faith in yourself is strong, and nothing can bend it, the right people and the right moments will start aligning for you.

However, your faith in yourself is the trigger point; it is the catalyst to everything else lining up. If your faith in yourself is swayed, what good is it to convince others to believe in you? Because when you believe in yourself, then your light within shines brightly. You will only need to speak your truth, and you will have believers and followers.

---

## *Destiny is a collection of choices, decisions, commitments, and submissions you make throughout your life.*

---

Destiny is less of an end goal and more of a path in life. You have to realize that life energy is flowing, it's moving, and it's pulsating. You are a vibrating being. There is no end goal because you are moving forward every second to something. Even by not doing anything, you are doing something that affects the choices you make in life.

Some beings think of destiny as the sum of everything you do in life. However, while you are alive, destiny is still a moving force for you. And when you leave this world, then destiny means nothing to you. So in a matter-of-fact statement– destiny is a collective flow of actions you make daily that lead you from one place to another.

Instead of relying on some words for directing your destiny, take count of your internal temperature and how your outlook in life impacts your future. When it rains, what do you say, do, feel? When you miss the bus, what do you say, do, and feel? Whatever you say, do, and feel impacts your body's energy level, and that diverts your movement, thought, and feeling thereon after. You probably have heard, " this day is off to a bad start," can you see this is such a negative way to project one action to the actions of the entire day? You then, by your low vibration, have impacted the future activities of that day. When are you going to stop?

You spilled coffee on your coat, you missed the morning bus, the fellow you sat with was not giving you enough space on the bus, and then you get to the appointment, and they tell you they need to reschedule– you only have one choice if you want to feel good about yourself! To turn this around, you are just a thought away. You can smile, take a deep breath, and carry on.

If you choose to hold a grudge against your day, do you think anyone else cares? The hard truth is nobody cares. You will be burning in your misery alone. So choose the alternative. Because in doing so lies the path to peace within yourself, and your destiny for every day, when you lay down to slumber, is to feel at peace. Peace for your actions, peace with your interactions, and peace with giving the day your full energy. When you give every moment your mindful energy, you are already on the path, and come rain or shine; your energy will take you through everything you are confronted with.

## Exercise

What has your typical bad day looked like up to this moment?

________________________________________

________________________________________

________________________________________

________________________________________

As it happens in everyones life, some days our inner light shines bright and we do not let one bad incident turn our entire day miserable. Do you have some examples from your life? Think back, I am sure you have buried in your memory.

________________________________________

________________________________________

________________________________________

________________________________________

What had happened on those days where your inner light was shining brighter?

________________________________________

________________________________________

________________________________________

What can you do to make that light shine brighter everyday or more often?

_______________________________

_______________________________

_______________________________

_______________________________

Make a promise to yourself to shine your light brighter, to not only brighten your path but to be a human light bulb brightening others path too.

I [your name] promise to:

_______________________________

_______________________________

_______________________________

_______________________________

# Chapter Seven

# Self-Mastery

Self-Mastery– the two words that have baffled many world leaders. It is safe to say that leading oneself and others is a lesson in self-mastery.

What is Self-Mastery?

Self is the I, me, myself. Mastery is a deep understanding of my needs, desires, addictions, neuroses, and the ability or wisdom to discern the choices that allow us to maintain self-control through self-regulation on our tendencies. In self-mastery, there is an awareness of a strength or a weakness, a determination to uncover the root cause, and the discipline to use one's free will to make choices to improve one's life.

Put simply, if sugar is bad for my health, I need

to curb my desire for sugary sweet food so that I am healthy. If I am addicted to alcohol, and it is damaging my life and relationships, am I aware that there is a problem? If I want to continue to better my life and recover my relationships, I need to do everything it takes to keep alcohol out of my life. If I realize that I am addicted to shopping to replace an emptiness in my life, then I need to keep my credit card at home when I go shopping and only take cash. These are some examples of how self-mastery works.

*Self-mastery is an awareness of a strength or a weakness, a determination to uncover the root cause, and the discipline to use one's free will to make choices to improve one's life.*

How often have we seen our leaders' lack of self-mastery impact our lives? Whether you are leading a country, team, family, or self, your ability to understand yourself and your triggers means you can live with mindfulness, knowing that your actions impact others' lives, whether directly or indirectly.

Look in your community and local news. How often have you seen the news about someone in power involved in a scam, scandal, or fraud when that individual held a prominent place in society? But also in ordinary day-to-day households, adults' actions, such as cheating, addictions, anger towards self and/or others, cause harm to the other family members. The children pay the ultimate sacrifice of being helpless victims of the action or inaction of the adults like we suffer through the actions and inactions of our leaders.

Self-mastery is not a new thing. Have you read about the Stanford Marshmallow Experiment about delayed gratification? If you have not, a simple web search will enlighten you to experiments similar to this, with newer online videos popping up to see if children or even pets can resist the temptation of instant gratification.

## *Self-mastery is about discipline, self-control, self-regulation, and self-awareness.*

One of the most straightforward lessons in self-mastery is that if something is in front of you does not mean you need to use it; try it, take it, eat it, etc. Self-mastery is about discipline, self-control, self-regulation, and self-awareness. It is about having an intimate relationship with your neuroses to the point of awareness right when you get that thought of it happening. For an alcohol addiction, as an example, that would mean the desire to have just one drink, which leads to the next and the next. To a shopaholic pressing that button for online shopping without seeing the money leaving your account is a lie that gets one deeper into debt. To the leader in an organization, raising their voice to get things done their way will mean they will continue to raise their voice until they end up doing it to the wrong person, which leads to their career demise.

To the person who continues to make a racist or sexist joke, apologies after being confronted mean it is already too late because their ongoing behavior means they were comfortable saying and doing actions that eventually caught up to them. People make mistakes. That's just part of being human. But mistakes have consequences, and there is a price someone pays.

---

### *People make mistakes. That's just part of being human.*

---

Self-mastery does not have a starting point. It can start anywhere on a person's timeline. For example, it could be after being called out for one's behavior one works to self-correct. Still, the essence of self-mastery is in understanding the consequences of your actions before your actions or inactions impact others and having a bird's eye view of the entire situation play out in your mind before you put yourself in deep water or blurt out something or do an action physically.

## Release Yourself From The Prison Of Your Own Making

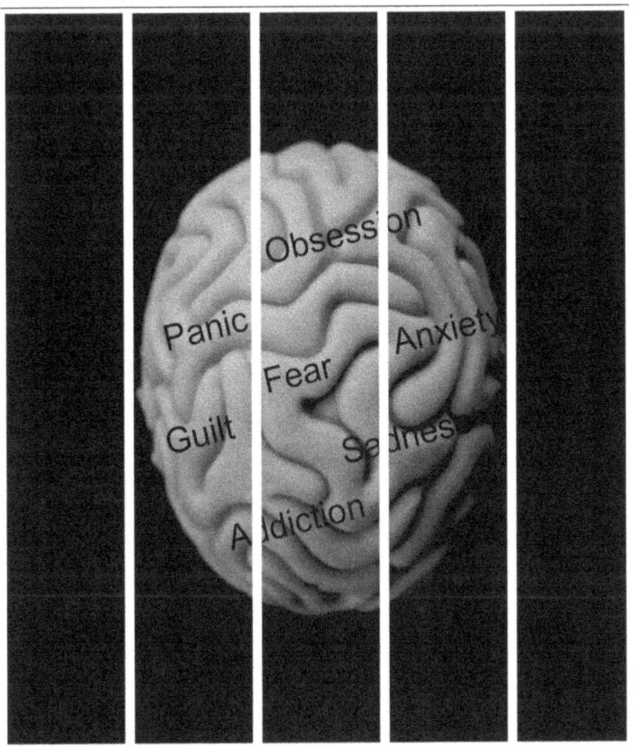

## Exercise

Whether we openly acknowledge it or not, we all in some part know our neuroses. What are your addictions and neuroses?

_______________________________________________

_______________________________________________

_______________________________________________

_______________________________________________

How did they originate?

_______________________________________________

_______________________________________________

_______________________________________________

List each one below and how you can self-regulate your addictions and neuroses:

_____  ___________________________________

_____  ___________________________________

_____  ___________________________________

_____  ___________________________________

_____  ___________________________________

Remember: the first step of self-mastery is to acknowledge your addictions and neuroses.

Name it.

Then you can heal it.

*You are loved. Every action you take to heal yourself, to do the inner self work is not benign. One day you will look back and you will see how far you have come.*

# Chapter Eight

# Healing

Over the years, we have learned that teaching is not limited to the classroom, and education is significantly underrated as a product of others' experiences used to inform another's learning. By now, we know that anything and anyone around us can teach us if we pay attention. If the message resonates with what we are going through, that moment or conversation becomes a teacher, lesson, and a learning opportunity.

The same applies to healing. In many parts of the world, going to therapy is not an option simply because paying others to give advice or listen to one's problem is not seen as appropriate. In the western world, insurance coverages give allowance for therapy services. I want to say that you should not feel bad about not wanting to go to therapy. You should also not feel bad about not being able to go to therapy. Many western movies show going to a therapist as a way to a successful life where you have talked to someone about your past traumas and come out with a new awareness and new outlook on life. I want to tell you that your life is not a movie, and you do not need to feel incomplete.

Cultural and social upbringing can make talking to outsiders challenging. But nothing stands in the way of you to quieten your mind and listen to your body and heart. Your body always knows, problems occur when you avoid listening to what it says.

---

### *Your body always knows, problems occur when you avoid listening to what it says.*

---

In places where there is no therapist, do you think people do not work through their issues? Not at all.

Therapy is one way to heal, but it is not the only way.

Healing requires one to go within. It requires an intimate knowledge of one's own fears, traumas, and perceived limitations. Healing requires honesty with self. You can tell others what they want to hear, but you know what really is bothering you. You know what keeps you awake at two o'clock in the morning in the pitch black of the night and in pin-drop silence. You know the truth of why you are the way you are.

You know your public face and private face. Healing requires you to make friends with your private face that you do not show anyone at all. With this kind of relationship, you can start noticing blockages in your life and address them.

If you have done this in the past, you can relate to what I will say next. And I can assure you that we all have done this. Have you in the past asked for others' opinions on something, knowing quite well that you already know the answer or the next step. Still, you do not want to take that next step, and so you are hoping others will say the opposite, and so you do not have to listen to what your body is telling you.

Healing requires trust with self. Moreover, trust requires listening to that inner knowing within all of us, known as the gut feeling.

## *Healing requires trust with self.*

When you are on your deathbed, only you can recall the events of the past all the way from your childhood to your current situation, and only you can truly understand your journey. No amount of lying to yourself will make any impact on your life. Like a knitter or a crocheter needs to untangle a ball of yarn patiently. Similarly, to heal yourself, you need to patiently address each blockage and open yourself up for an honest interaction with all your wounded parts.

## Exercise

What keeps you awake at night?

_______________________________________________

_______________________________________________

_______________________________________________

_______________________________________________

What have you done about thoughts that keep you awake at night?

_______________________________________________

_______________________________________________

_______________________________________________

_______________________________________________

Knowing what you know now, what steps can you take today to make peace with yourself so that you can sleep knowing you did your best?

_______________________________________________

_______________________________________________

_______________________________________________

_______________________________________________

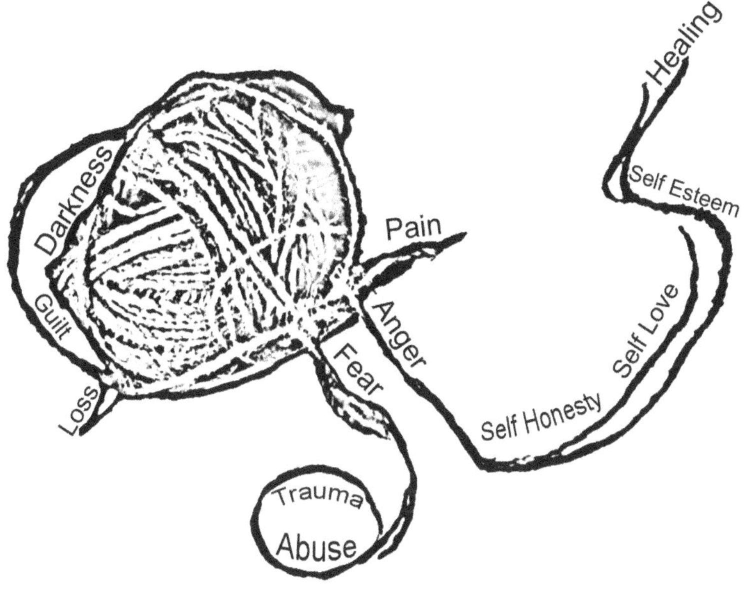

Healing
Self Esteem
Self Love
Self Honesty
Darkness
Guilt
Loss
Pain
Anger
Fear
Trauma
Abuse

# Chapter Nine

# You are Powerful

Y ou have in you everything. The entire Universe and its secrets live in you. You are the manifestor. You are the healer. You are divinely connected to all eternity; the past, the present, and the future. With so much power, why are you afraid of the impact you can have in this world?

Why are you choosing to live small? Forgive your early childhood caregivers and how they raised you to know your place in this world because they were also taught to dim their light by their caregivers. Knowing what you know now, what can you not do?

Knowing that the entire cosmos lives inside you, as a divine being who possesses the power to tap into the secrets of the Universe, answer these questions:

How do you choose to live?

_______________________________________

_______________________________________

_______________________________________

_______________________________________

What do you choose to do for work?

_______________________________________

_______________________________________

_______________________________________

_______________________________________

How do you contribute to the world?

_______________________________________

_______________________________________

_______________________________________

_______________________________________

Let us talk about this idea of duality that we have; some people believe that there are physical, emotional, and mental aspects of life. I want to extend the conversation to the spiritual realm. On the physical level, let us say you have your banks, schools, house, family, and friends. In order to be successful and a well-rounded person, you must do certain things in life. Such as, as a child, you need to go to school. When you are five or six years old, you start going to kindergarten.

After that, you go to grade school, then through high school, and so forth to become a productive contributing citizen to provide for yourself and your family.

Then on the emotional level, we experience love, hate, fear, sadness, anger, joy, etc. On the emotional level, we also feel connections, attachments, detachments that either make us happy or sad, or a myriad of other feelings that cause us to feel love or absence of love or fear or lack thereof. We must learn how to cope with these emotions healthily so that they do not control our lives.

## *Our thoughts and beliefs guide our actions and decisions.*

On the mental level, our thoughts and beliefs guide our actions and decisions. We learn how to think critically and rationally so that we can make sound choices in life. On the mental level, we find reasons for justifying our feelings, events in our lives, patterns of behavior, and resulting outcomes. The mental level is how we justify the incidents and occurrences in life. We all try to justify how our lives play out because then we have no excuse for what happens to us, what we let happen to us, or simply because we need to blame ourselves, others, or the situations so we can move forward in life. However, there is a key step we ignore, overlook, or forget that it exists– the spiritual realm– and from that perspective– we have life lessons.

The spiritual realm is not about doing but about being. It is about who you are as a person, not what you do. When you are tuned into your spiritual realm, you are in touch with your true self. You are connected to something larger than yourself. As a result, you have a sense of peace and calm. You know who you are and what you want in life. You are living in the present moment and not worrying about the past or the future. You are living in love and compassion.

One can say there comes a softness in your way of being. When you are connected to your spiritual self, you realize that we are all connected and that we are all one. We are all connected to the same source of Energy. This is the Energy that created the Universe and everything in it. We are all made of the same stuff. The atoms and molecules that make up our bodies are the same atoms and molecules that make up the stars and planets. We are all interconnected and interdependent.

---

> ## *When you are connected to your spiritual self, you realize that we are all connected and that we are all one.*

---

What happens to one of us happens to all of us. The spiritual realm is about unity, not separation. It is about oneness, not duality. We are all one with the Energy that created us. When we realize this, we can tap into the power of this Energy and use it to heal ourselves and the world around us. In the spiritual realm is where we connect with our higher selves, god/ goddess/ universe/ source energy/ etc. Through tapping into the spiritual realm, we find our purpose and meaning in life. This is where we heal ourselves emotionally and mentally so that we can live our best lives physically.

So what level are you functioning on and why?

_______________________________________________

_______________________________________________

_______________________________________________

_______________________________________________

Are you balanced or imbalanced?

_______________________________________________

_______________________________________________

_______________________________________________

What steps do you need to take to achieve balance in your life?

_______________________________________________

_______________________________________________

_______________________________________________

I want you to think of everything that happened to you and is happening to you from the spiritual perspective.

But how? You may ask.

Although many of you do not see spirits, you know that something exists beyond the physical realm. For example, many of us have heard and believe that dogs and cats can hear and see things before they happen. In addition, there are many stories from end-of-life care nurses who also attest to the unexplainable occurrences before someone passes the earthly plane, such as the smell of death in the room. Alternatively, how about this, when you feel someone's vibe is off from yours and you have a gut-wrenching feeling that you need to protect yourself, or when you connect with someone you just met and felt like you have known them forever?

*The higher power is always giving us signs and nudges; however, it is up to us whether we listen to them or not. The key is to be open to recognizing them and trust that whatever message we receive is for our highest good.*

All of these examples point to a higher power or energy source that is constantly interacting with us. Some may call it God, Source Energy, Universe, or simply Love. This higher power is always giving us signs and nudges; however, it is up to us whether we listen to them or not. The key is to be open to recognizing them and trust that whatever message we receive is for our highest good. So, the next time you have a feeling or sense about something, pay attention to it and see what happens. You may be surprised at how accurate your intuition is!

It is difficult to explain the spiritual realm to those who have not experienced it for themselves. It is a realm of Energy and consciousness that goes beyond the physical world. In order to understand the spiritual realm, one must have faith, trust, intuition, and an inner knowing. This inner knowing is what guides us on our spiritual journey. We are all connected to the same pool of consciousness, and we all have lessons to learn in this lifetime. The spiritual realm is much grander than the physical world, and it is filled with love, light, and wisdom. When we connect with our higher selves, we are able to tap into this infinite wisdom and understanding. We are all on a journey back to the source of our being, and the spiritual realm is a beautiful place to begin that journey. We are all connected on a deep level. When we help others, we are helping ourselves. When we love others, we are loving ourselves. We are all One.

Many of us are caught up in what we see in the physical world because we think that seeing is believing. Seeing is not always believing. Just because you cannot see something does not mean it is not there. The spiritual realm is a perfect example of this. The spiritual realm is all around us, but we must be open to it to see it. It is a different way of looking at things. We must be willing to let go of our preconceived notions and open our minds to new possibilities. Only then can we begin to see the spiritual realm manifest and we begin to understand that it is all around us.

The spiritual realm is just as "real" as the physical level. It is more real, in fact. The physical world is an illusion; it is not permanent. The spiritual world is permanent. It is eternal. It is the only reality. For example, in the Bhagavad Gita, Krishna says, when we die, our Spirit leaves our physical body and goes to the spiritual realm. The physical world disappears; it ceases to exist for us. Therefore, focusing on the spiritual realm is much more important than the physical realm. To experience lasting happiness, you must connect with the Spirit within you and the Spirit that pervades the Universe. You must live in harmony with Spirit. You must align your will with the will of the Universe. When you do this, you will experience true bliss, far greater than anything the physical world can offer.

## *We are all on a journey back to the source of our being.*

But, is there enough?

There is always competition, whether we like it or not. We are constantly fighting and competing with others because we feel like there are limited resources. If you have worked in the corporate world or had a job in an organization, many of you know that there is always competition. Many people believe that in order to succeed because there is a limited amount of resources to go around, we need to do better than the other person to get to where we are going. Even though you may not intentionally do it, there is always this human nature that we are competing with others. We think that on the physical level, one needs to compete for the object of our desire. If one pushes others down, that is just the nature of the survival of the fittest mentality, believing there is not much to go around. However, we are more than just our physical bodies. We are spiritual beings here on this Earth learning our earthly lessons. There is more to life than just the physical realm. There is an infinite supply of Energy, love, and abundance available to us. We just need to open ourselves up to receive it. When we live from this higher perspective, we can start to create our reality from a place of love instead of fear. When we do that, we can begin to change the world around us. We need to remember that we are all connected. We are all one. When we harm another, we are harming ourselves. When we help another, we are helping ourselves. We need to learn to love and support each other instead of competing with each other. Only then can we truly succeed in life.

In the spiritual realm, as I mentioned earlier, life exists on a grander scale. Because we come from a pool of consciousness, we naturally have everything we need for our earthly journey. Furthermore, there exists a law of greater good and the power of positive thinking and prayers to achieve what we need on the earth plane. We see this once in a while, especially when a group of people gather to pray because something tragic happened, or a group of people praying for a person's healing or praying for World Peace. When people come in prayer, usually, it is because a group of people who understand the idea of kindness, compassion, and empathy and its impact on the spiritual level to get what is yours by the mere fact that your soul chose to be born to experience this Earth. So, you need to ensure that you are of a positive mind, kind, not putting anyone down, and not pushing anyone into a corner just because you need to move ahead.

## *We are spiritual beings here on this Earth learning our earthly lessons.*

On the spiritual level, it is believed that there is always enough for everyone. This is because the world was created with abundance already available. For example, the Bible says that everything we need was created at the beginning, meaning that it exists on a spiritual plane. In order to receive what we desire, we need to ensure that our thoughts, dreams, visions, and actions are all aligned. If our thoughts contradict our dreams, we will not be able to achieve what we want. The Law of Attraction states that we attract what we put our focus on. We will attract more lack into our lives if we focus on lack. If however, we focus on abundance, we will attract more abundance. This is because the Universe is abundant, and there is always more than enough to go around. For example, if we think that we do not deserve authentic love, we will not be able to find a partner who can give us that love.

Therefore, we need to operate from a place of abundance in order to receive what we desire. The key is to align our thoughts, dreams, and actions with our aspirations. This means doing the opposite of what we are often told to do in the physical world. We are told to compete with others instead of cooperating, for example. Instead, we should focus on cooperating and working together so that everyone can achieve their desires. By operating from a place of abundance, we can create a world where everyone has what they need to lead happy and fulfilled lives. Moreover, when we manifest our desires, not only do we get what we want, but we also help to create abundance for others as well. So it is not just about attracting what we want for ourselves but about creating abundance for all.

*The key is to align our thoughts, dreams, and actions with our aspirations.*

We are all on our own exclusive spiritual journey as a result of our own soul contracts. Though it may sometimes feel like we are in competition with others, striving to be better or more "spiritual" than them, the truth is that the only person we are in competition with is ourselves. Therefore, our goal should be to improve our own physical, emotional, and mental state to become the best version of ourselves that we can be. This is not an easy task, but it is one that is well worth striving for. When we are kind and compassionate to ourselves, it naturally follows that we will treat others in the same way. So let us strive to be positive and accepting of ourselves and others, knowing that we are all on a journey to becoming the best that we can be.

If you believe in yourself, you are tapping into a much larger power. You are tapping into the power of the Universe itself. When you realize that you are not just a tiny speck in the grand scheme of things but, in reality, a fundamental part of the puzzle, you can start to see how vital your role truly is. If everyone believed in themselves as much as they should, the world would be a completely different place. We would all be working together towards a common goal instead of fighting tooth and nail against each other. Imagine what we could accomplish if we all realized our potential and acted on it. Only then can we hope to make a real difference in the world.

If you believe in yourself, your birthright, your inheritance, and your heritage from the divine sacred Universe, that took care of you from before you were even conceived, you can affirm that:

### *Affirmation*

*I believe that I deserve*
*___________ because I am a part*
*of the universal consciousness; I*
*am meant to have abundance; I am*
*meant to live life with ease; I am*
*meant to have a successful life.*

On a similar level regarding financial goals, because there are many different belief systems on the physical level and each one of us has different life lessons we came to learn, not everyone can learn the same thing because there are many different paths and lessons. It is so easy to look at our physical environment and think this is what our lot is. However, in your mind– the mind which is connected to the spiritual world, you cannot see the mind; you can see the brain; and likewise, you can see the heart, but you cannot see emotion; you can feel emotion– so similar to that, on the spiritual level, when you without any doubt, believe in your mind that there is a bank, like a wishing well you may have heard of as a child, so to speak, there is an abundant bank that which will give me whatever it is that I want, then you are on your path.

## *Imagine what we could accomplish if we all realized our potential and acted on it.*

So when it comes to financial goals, or any goals for that matter, it is essential to realize that it is up to each individual to create their own reality. If you believe that you can manifest whatever it is you desire, you will be able to do so. It is all about aligning your thoughts and feelings with your desired outcome. When you are in alignment, anything and everything is possible. So if your goal is to achieve financial abundance, start by believing that it is possible and that you are worthy of achieving it. Then take steps towards achieving your goal and watch as your life transforms before your eyes. All things are possible when you open your mind and heart to limitless possibilities.

In summary, anything that you want or need is already available to you in the spiritual realm. Just as you have adventures in the physical world, you can have similar adventures in the spiritual world. The spiritual world is just as real as the physical world even though you can not see it with your physical eyes. In order to connect with the spiritual realm, you need to tune in to your heart, your breath, your gut– the seat of your intuition– and your mind. Think of the spiritual world as a grand adventure; do not be afraid to think big. Be willing to Believe in Abundance.

*Anything that you want or need is already available to you in the spiritual realm.*

Whatever you want on the spiritual level, you must think of it in grandiose terms; they never run out like grocery stores run out of your favorite food. It is on a larger-than-life level, and anything that you need is already available in that level of existence in the Universe on the spirit level. You do not need to compete with anyone or struggle to get what you want. You do not need to push anyone down; you do not need to struggle or compete with others. You just need to be a human being with compassion and empathy, not just for others but also for yourself. You must also believe that you were not sent to this Earth to suffer. By doing so, you open yourself to possibilities on the spiritual plane beyond your wildest dreams. So tune inward; explore the spiritual world, and see what amazing adventures await you.

If you learn this lesson, you are on your path to success, whatever success is for you. When I say, whatever success is for you, what I am saying is not what you think based on your current situation in the physical realm; I am saying focus on what it is that you want. Success is a difficult concept to define. The path to success is not always easy to see. There can be obstacles in our way that cloud our vision and make it difficult to move forward. Sometimes we need to be reminded that our current situation is not permanent and that we have the power to create our own reality. When we focus on what we want rather than what we have, we open ourselves up to limitless possibilities. If we learn the lesson of looking beyond these obstacles and focusing on our goals, we can find the strength to continue on our journey.

For some, success might mean financial security. For others, it might mean personal fulfillment; for others still, it might mean making a difference in the world. Whatever success is for you, one thing is certain: if you want to achieve it, you need to learn the lessons that will lead you there. One of the most important lessons you can learn is to focus on what you want rather than on your current circumstances. It can be easy to get caught up in the daily grind and forget what you are striving for. However, if you take the time to visualize where you want to be and to focus your energy on getting there, you will be much more likely to achieve your goals.

Another important lesson is to keep your spiritual bank account full. This means ensuring that your thoughts, words, and actions align with your highest ideals. When you do this, you open yourself up to receive all good things. So if you want to experience success in whatever form it takes for you, make sure to learn these essential lessons. By doing so, you will be well on your way to achieving your dreams. The spiritual bank is always open and ready to give us whatever we desire. All we need to do is ask. If we keep this in mind, we will always find our way to success.

## *Believe in Abundance.*

I know some of you will be phuzzled[1] and thinking– But how can I talk about what I want when I have this or that current situation?

Instead of looking at where you are, think about where you want to be. Create that mentality, create that image in your mind, and know that the spiritual bank is open to giving you whatever you want.

You also must remember that this spiritual bank will give you whatever you want without any input

---

1       Words: Phuzzled- pronunciation (fuh-zeld)
Definition:  puzzled and fuzzy on any concept that may seem unreal or beyond your current conceptual mind to comprehend.

from it– no universal father is stopping you from using the fire to heat your house or burning it to the ground. Let us just call it a Spiritual Yes! Bank. Whether you say I want poverty or I want success, the Spiritual Yes! Bank is going to give it to you. At this Spiritual Yes! Bank, you do not need to be or have any color, religion, race, caste, or belief system restriction. You, by your birthright of being a human with a mind, can think whatever you want.

Furthermore, you have the wisdom to discern what you want. You can affirm: I am happy, and the Universe responds: Yes! You can say I am stupid Universe says yes. You say I am brilliant; the Universe says yes. If you repeat, I am (…add anything after that…) and carry a belief that you are that; you will manifest that for yourself. You have the choice to use your thoughts and words to create the life you want. That makes you powerful. Use that choice wisely.

Remember:

> ***To manifest anything in your life,
> you must wholeheartedly believe that
> which you want is already yours, like
> you believe that __________ (say
> your first name) is your name.***

(You know, when someone shouts a name, and it is your name, you look around to see who is saying your name– you believe that they are calling your name- it may also be someone else's name. But, nevertheless, you still look anyway because you know that is the name your earthly caregivers call you by. So, I want you to put that much faith in whatever you desire to manifest).

You truly are powerful. It is time that you believe that!

YES BANK

# Chapter Ten

# You are a Vibrational Being

It is your responsibility to do the best for yourself in life. You cannot force anyone else in your family, in your friends' circle, or in your community to elevate their life; you are where you are as a result of your thought and action, and you need to elevate your vibration or your thought to get to the next level. You are not responsible for anybody else in your circle; everybody is a  protagonist in their own life. With persistence and the choices they make, they are going to move up or down, forward or backward, as per the limit they have set on their consciousness.

You are only responsible for how you fit into this cycle of life. It is a universal law that we reap what we sow. If we want to elevate our lives, it starts with us making better choices. Every thought and action we take is planting a seed. It's up to us to decide what kind of seeds we want to plant. Remember, it is not our job to make the choices for others, but rather to lead by example and hope that they follow suit. So let's Elevate our thought, Elevate our vibrations, and Elevate our lives!

If you are in a situation where you were working on your thought, and you are reading all the self-help books or listening to an audio recording, etc., that you are thinking will better your life, and then you try to push it on other people, which I know I have done.

There have been times when I have sent an email link to someone for a video or even bought a book and sent it to someone. I actually sent it to many someones and then got upset because I was thinking, "You know here I am, spending money, buying and sending you this;  I know this is best, but why are you not reading this?" or "I bought it for you, and you are not taking this chance to do the right thing, and by reading this you can better your situation, and because you know I am doing that too so I think that we are on the same page; so let me inspire you because when I am talking about it to you, and I see you show interest which I assume as you feeling inspired, so I think let me send you a book or let me do this or that."

It is like saying that you can take the horse to the water, but you can not make it drink. So I have realized that every individual plays a leading role in their own life, and they have to do things their way to find what will work for them.

You are not responsible for your circle of friends, your family, or your community. You are not responsible for elevating anyone else, and neither are you to cause any harm to others; let me make this clear. You are responsible for your mental pitter-patter. You are responsible for raising your vibration, and your consciousness. This is important to say that it does not matter who your friendship circle, your love circle, or your community is.

When you raise your vibration, the universe is going to pick you from where you are and place you in an environment that is actually in the same level of consciousness equivalent to where you are vibrationally. You are not responsible for a community of people. You cannot raise your vibration and think that you will take a community or a circle of people with you to another level. Everybody has their own journey to pursue.

*You are responsible for raising your vibration, and your consciousness.*

Your responsibility in this life is to increase your vibration so that you will be placed in an environment that will be equivalent to where you are in your consciousness. It is like when you have been listening to a channel on the radio. It does not mean that everybody in your friends or family is going to be listening to that same channel, and so if you are listening to a song on a particular channel and you are thinking that your friendship circle or your family are listening to the same thing– that's pure madness. People have different tastes, styles, and preferences, and they may be listening to something else, so how can they understand what you are listening to when they are only tuned in to what they are inspired by.

More specifically, have you ever wondered why some people just "get" you while others just don't quite understand what makes you tick? Those who "get" you is because you're vibrating at a frequency that is in alignment with their own. So, if you want to attract more people, experiences, and circumstances into your life that are in alignment with who you really are and what you want out of life. It is important to do the inner work necessary to increase your vibration. This means becoming more aware of your thoughts, emotions, and actions, and working on letting go of anything that is holding you back from living your best life. When you vibrate at a higher frequency, you will naturally attract more of what you desire into your life.

---

## *You are the only one responsible for changing your mental attitude.*

---

You are only responsible for changing your mental attitude; this includes your thoughts and beliefs about who you are, what you desire, what you expect and deserve, and what is the best in life for you– whatever your best is.  Your mental attitude is everything. It includes your thoughts and beliefs about who you are, what you desire, what you expect and deserve, what is the best in life for you, and whatever your best is.

When you change your mental attitude, it changes your life experiences. The better you feel about yourself, the more likely you are to experience good things happening to you. It's not just positive thinking; it's knowing that you deserve the best and making sure your thoughts and beliefs reflect that. When you truly believe that you are worthy of the best life has to offer, manifestation will occur more readily and easily. So take responsibility for your mental attitude and watch your life change for the better.

Everybody has different ideas of what is best. And that's okay! What matters most is that you understand your own desires. Once you do, you'll start to believe that you already have everything you need. You do not need to be scared, you do not need to be stressed. The universe has a funny way of putting us in the same state of mind and surrounding us with similar people whenever we are vibrating at the same frequency.

It is like tuning into a radio station: you cannot be listening to a channel and thinking that you will hear something else because that channel only has a specific type of tune, talks, or music for a particular group of clientele. You have to be open to other frequencies if you want to expand your horizons. So do not be afraid to tune your "vibrational" channel to align to your goals. You will find what it is you dream, think about, and envision. That is the law. You will manifest what you constantly think about. Try it!

## Exercise

Have you ever accidentally manifested something? (Explain)

_______________________________________________

_______________________________________________

_______________________________________________

_______________________________________________

What were you feeling, and thinking when you accidentally manifested?

_______________________________________________

_______________________________________________

_______________________________________________

## Manifest

How would you like to intentionally manifest?

Remember, for this to happen, you have to ensure that your thoughts, actions, and feelings match. You have to be in the state of contentment that your desire already exists etherically. You must feel you deserve this desire of yours to show up in your physical life. Imagine that you already have what it is you desire and go about your day (s) as you already have it. Think of it, dream of it, and visualize what it is like to hold your desired result in your physical presence. And know that if you do not have what you desire it's because there exists in you doubt that you are not worthy of that which you desire.

We are each capable of attracting our heart's desire into our lives. In order to do this, we must first get clear about what it is we want to attract. Once we know what we want, we can begin to take steps to manifest it. This requires that our beliefs, behaviors, and emotions all match our desired outcome. For example, if we want to attract abundance into our lives, we must believe that we are deserving of abundance. We must also take action steps to achieve our goal, such as setting up a business, going to school, or investing, etc. Finally, we must be in the emotional state of contentment that comes from knowing that our desired outcome is on its way.

By aligning our thoughts, actions, and feelings with our visualizations, we can create the conditions necessary for manifestation to occur. The ability to manifest what you desire is within each and every one of us. The key to making it happen is to ensure that your thoughts, actions, and feelings are all aligned with your desired outcome. This means believing that you deserve to have what you want, and visualizing yourself already in possession of it. When you can do this, you send a powerful message to the Universe that will help to attract your desire into your physical reality. Remember, doubt is the enemy of manifestation, so always focus on maintaining faith that you will achieve your goal. With a little practice, you'll be manifesting all the abundance you desire in no time!

### Experiment: Baby Steps….

Manifest a cup of coffee, a friend reaching out to you, a message for you from the universe as lyrics from a song or a sign on a building, ….the ideas are endless, be creative. As you receive the messages, become in tune with yourself and watch your life change. Warning: you must not use manifestation to intend harm on anyone as it will manifest in your own life. Also, you can not use manifestation to make someone do something for you if it is not their free will. Remember that everybody has free will. So choose to make your life better. Focus only on yourself. It is not selfish. You can not change others, you can only change your life.

As you become attuned to the messages of the universe, you will find that your life begins to change for the better. The law of attraction dictates that like attracts like. So, by focusing on positive thoughts and intentions, you will begin to see more positive results in your life. This is not to say that everything will be perfect all of the time. However, you will find that you are better able to handle whatever challenges come your way when you are focused on manifesting a positive life. Remember, you have the power to change your life for the better. Focus only on yourself and watch your life transform.

## Exercise

What will you manifest?

_______________________________________________

_______________________________________________

_______________________________________________

_______________________________________________

## Experiment: Increasing your Vibration

So, how can you start increasing your vibration today? One way is by practicing gratitude. Every time you focus on what's good in your life– no matter how small– you are increasing your vibration. Take a few moments each day to reflect on the things, people, and experiences in your life that make you feel good. Another way to increase your vibration is by spending time in nature. Connecting with the natural world helps to ground and center you, raising your vibration in the process. So get outside as often as possible, and take time to appreciate the beauty that surrounds you. Yet another way to increase your vibration is to be in a state of love for any experience you encounter that used to trigger you. Love every action and interaction. Love every fear thought, lack thought. Give love to every moment of weakness, and struggle you are confronted with. Send loving intention to every upset and angry person, or situation you are confronted with.

As soon as you realize something is causing a feeling that is not coming from a place of love, recognize that, breathe deeply and notice how you feel when your higher self intervenes to transmute the initial feeling into love. Until you learn to operate from the place of love, pay attention to moments that frustrate you.

Breathe in and out. Pause. Reset. Then continue what you were doing.

By making an effort to increase your vibration on a daily basis, you will begin to create more of the life that you truly desire. And isn't that what we all ultimately want?

### Exercise

What are you going to do today to increase your vibration?

___________________________________________

___________________________________________

___________________________________________

___________________________________________

Learn from Nature, We are Beautiful Just the Way We Are.

# Chapter Eleven

# Forgiveness

Forgiveness is the ability to let go of memories that no longer serve you. Forgiving is an aspect of healing because it symbolizes the freedom to process incidents and situations in which you let yourself down by assessing incorrectly.

Forgiveness is an act of kindness, empathy, choice, and free will. It is a choice that frees up the space in your mind held up by guilt and anger to create room for empathy, grace, creativity, inspiration, and freedom of movement to move on with the intention to let go and self-correct behaviors that no longer serve you. When you forgive, you are essentially saying "I choose to let go of this memory so that I can be free." It is a choice that allows you to take back control of your life and create the space necessary for healing.

---

## *Forgiveness is the ability to let go of memories that no longer serve you.*

---

It is essential to understand that while you are holding onto anger, grudge, insult, and betrayal, you do not have any space to get past those pains. Granted that there are people who have genuinely hurt you at a time in space; however, holding onto those incidents in your mind and replaying them repeatedly is like picking at a wound right when the scab is forming; or not even letting the scab form because you keep rubbing the wound raw.

Imagine if you do not let this scab form, and you keep on rubbing the sore. Do you think it will ever heal? When we hold onto these negative emotions, we are not only re-living the pain of the original hurt, but we are also preventing ourselves from moving forward. What I described about a physical wound is a metaphysical manifestation of memories that no longer serve you and how the memories fester and cause ailments in your body. In order to heal, we need to let go of the past and make room for new experiences. This can be a difficult process, but it is essential for our well-being. By forgiving those who have hurt us, we can finally start to heal the wounds of the past and move on with our lives.

When others hurt us, we tend to believe what

they say without thinking twice that maybe they are acting out because they are hurt. We believe them because we want to belong. We want to be loved. We want to be understood. Others hurt us because we are vulnerable, and we let whatever they say touch the core of our being. This is especially true when we are children, and our caregivers say things that we start to believe about ourselves and then carry those beliefs into adulthood. It creates a disconnect between our reality and what identity we hold about ourselves in our lives. In adulthood, that specific hurt shows up in our relationships with someone who is trying to love us. Still, we may not believe that we are worthy of love.

---

> ***By forgiving those who have hurt us, we can finally start to heal the wounds of the past and move on with our lives.***

---

While others hurt us, the worst part of that hurting is that we continue to hurt ourselves. We beat ourselves up for not being aware, for not being smart enough to recognize incidents when others were hurting us, tricking us, or playing with our emotions. We replay incidents of guilt that we carry for not leaving a situation; we hurt ourselves for not recognizing someone's behavior that hurt us. We accept the guilt of things that happened in childhood even though, as children, we could not remove ourselves from situations, but instead of forgiving ourselves, we keep on punishing ourselves for incidents that were beyond our control.

The path to forgiveness requires the strength to let go of your insecurities and vulnerabilities; while acknowledging that the situation happened and recognizing that you are no longer in that situation.

### *Affirmation*

> ***I forgive myself and others, and I
> am holding space for what is next
> to come in my healing. I let go of
> anything that no longer serves me.  I
> am a good person. I attract goodness
> and kindness toward myself.***

Sometimes it is difficult to let go and forgive, especially others who have hurt us, but you must remember that forgiveness is not about others. It is about you and your own healing journey. You may think if I forgive them, then I may be perceived as a doormat, and they may hurt me again. There is a clear distinction between forgiveness and hurt. I am not telling you to be hurt again. You have the free will to decide to forgive others and create a boundary by your behavior and words that project to others that their behaviors are no longer acceptable.

Once you have forgiven others, you do not need to be talking to the person; if you know the nature of that person and you know that they will hurt you again; you do not need to interact with them as before. When the hurt initially happened, you did not have a boundary, you did not speak up, or you could not speak up for a myriad of reasons. But forgiveness is not about them. It never was about them. Forgiveness is about freeing yourself from the weight of others' negativity, insecurities, and other issues that we absorb and carry. Instead of thinking that what others do to us says a lot about them, we take it on as if we are to be blamed.

Forgive others for your own peace of mind.

---

*It is time you let go of the weight of the guilt and the heaviness and shame you carry that no longer serves you.*

---

I encourage you to think of forgiveness as a way to free yourself from the shackles of others' judgments, opinions, and beliefs about you. It is time you let go of the weight of the guilt and the heaviness and shame you carry that no longer serves you. Forgiving others and forgiving yourself means you are free to turn your life around and engage more holistically with the life energy buzzing all around you. You are no longer chained by the weight of others' thinking. You are no longer tied to the perception of others. Feel free to recreate your life the way you want it to be. You are free to live your life the way you want it.

Forgive your parents, for they were only trying to teach

you things they were taught, and they did not know any better.

Forgive your caregivers, for they were doing to you what they thought was best.

Forgive those that hurt you when you were a child, and you could not speak up for yourself.

Forgive those who have hurt you in your adulthood, for they were only replaying what their parents and caregivers taught them.

Most importantly, forgive yourself for holding onto those believes, mindsets, thought patterns, guilt, family pressures that made you believe that you had no choice in how you live your life.

Forgive yourself for believing that you were not enough.

Forgive yourself for not loving yourself.

Forgive yourself!

### *Affirmation*

*Softly: I am Free*

*Louder: I am Free*

*Louder: I am Free*

*Louder: I am Free*

# *Louder: I am Free*

# Chapter Twelve

# Recalibration

Recalibration is aligning your life to your higher self. When you grow spiritually, you vibrate at a higher state, perhaps different from your family or environment, which may cause discomfort if they are not aligned to their higher self. Vibrating at a higher self spiritually may look like:

- A new outlook on life
- A sudden realization that everything that happened to you was happening for you to grow to your higher potential
- A feeling of gratitude for everything that is coming in your life
- An awareness of your purpose on this earth or your life's mission
- Unexplained joy and acceptance of your life

journey, like finding all the puzzle pieces and seeing them connect with ease
- Delight in simple pleasure such as:
    - Spending time in nature
    - Spending time in contemplation
    - Eating clean, simple food that gives you clarity
    - Random tears of gratitude
    - A new found wakefulness to life you have never felt before
- A feeling of connection to the divine where messages to your questions appear in unexpected ways, such as numbers or names on street signs, repeatedly looking at the same number appearing in many different places, such as looking at the clock and seeing a number and hearing that same number on the radio or in a magazine and knowing that this is way too many signs of being mere coincidences.
- A sudden desire to re-invent your life such as:
    - Quiting your job / relationship, etc.
    - Moving to a new city, state, or country, with  an inner knowing and peace over your decision

Every change in your life is an opportunity to reclaim your self-mastery. The more you grow spiritually, the more you will notice elements of your life that are disconnected to your true self, such as: your job, your friend circle, the food you eat, and the acquaintances you have;  these can decrease or increase your connection to the divine in you. When you mindfully start looking at all areas of life, you get the opportunity to recalibrate and redesign your life to fit you. Just like weight gain and weight loss or your vision changes means you have to find the best fit of clothes or eyeglasses, recalibration means attuning to elements that enhance the new you.

Recalibration is not a one-time thing. Instead, it is an ongoing process to reinvent. Like the seasonal changes that bring newness into our lives, I am dedicating this last chapter to renewal, rejuvenation, recalibration, and reset. You have seen this in nature; after a storm, disaster, or any kind of traumatic incident, nature resets and renews itself for a fresh start. The same is required of us after a change in our lives. People celebrate major events such as births, marriages, deaths, and divorces as they bring significant change in their lives. The most common one is birthdays for having lived another year, which is a privilege not afforded to many.

> ***Recalibration is not a one-time thing. Instead, it is an ongoing process to reinvent.***

This same principle must be applied to victories in life that not everyone may know about. For instance, people coming out of domestic violence relationships make a major self change. For example, I cut my thigh-length hair to shoulder length to symbolize a new beginning when I got out of a traumatic four-year domestic violence relationship.

Recalibration is a mind, body, and soul experience because you have to involve all your wounded parts in going through the process of grieving, renewing, and reawakening to your higher self. Any time you recalibrate and shed something that was causing you grief, you are sloughing off parts of yourself that are not needed on your journey to the higher version of your Self.

*Any significant shift in life allows us the opportunity to reassess what is working, what is not working, what can be fixed, and what needs to be let go.*

Recalibration requires work. It requires you to face yourself with honesty and look at your life choices to determine what led you down this path. Coming home from a job that is toxic for you, pouring yourself a glass of wine, and putting on a face mask, is not self-care. It is skin care. Self-care requires growth and inner work. Do not label one thing as something else and call it good, while numbing yourself to the pains you have chosen to ignore. I am not saying that inner work is easy. It took me decades, and I am still working on myself.

Any significant shift in life allows us the opportunity to reassess what is working, what is not working, what can be fixed, and what needs to be let go. Do not be a person who is an emotional hoarder. Let go of what is not required on your self-growth journey.

Let go of the emotional baggage of pain that someone caused you. If it hasn't helped you till now, what are the chances that holding on to it will help you in the future? The emotional pain only causes you distress. When you choose to let go of the pain, you intentionally create space for more goodness to come in.

Your self-growth journey requires you to abandon anything that the higher version of yourself will not need. But think of it this way, when it is time to leave the earthly plane, it could be today, tomorrow, or whenever, all your collection of the best stuff is left as your soul continues. To let your old self die and the new self to be born, you need to let go of beliefs, people, pain, and trauma that kept you down and did not serve you. Yes, I said people because not everyone is going to continue on your life path with you. Only you are going to be the constant on your life path. Others will come to teach you a lesson, empower you, support your growth, and when you have learned your lesson, away they will go. Unfortunately, sometimes we get so caught up in our current situation that we repeat the same mistake with different people and expect different results.

Part of self-mastery is spending time thinking, sitting with yourself, talking to yourself, asking your higher self, "what is my lesson in this" "What is this situation trying to teach me?" "Why am I repeating the same mistake?" I promise you that if you spend enough time with your inner self in meditation, conversation, and playful engagement, you will find all the corners in your mind, body, and heart that you have shut away due to past traumas, disappointments, and other's expectations. As you gently listen to that inner voice, you will too find the universe speaking to you in signs, numbers, songs, written words, and a myriad of other ways that your divinity can connect with you.

I suggest that you intentionally create pockets of time in your day like you do for all your critical earthly decisions, rest in silence, ask the great universe to engage with, and most importantly, be alert to what you may have thought in the past to be coincidences to being synchronicities. You are not weird. You are not crazy. You are a divine being on this earth to learn your lesson and find out what human potential you are here to serve others with.

Lean into your softness and surrender yourself to the universe's calling. Learn to forgive yourself and others. Heal your wounded heart and rejoice in what brought you the most joy in your childhood. The universe is waiting with answers to all your questions. So listen, delight, and become the best version of yourself.

## Exercise

What are some of the synchronicities you have noticed in your life?

______________________________

______________________________

______________________________

______________________________

______________________________

______________________________

Did you tell anyone? y/n

What did they say?

______________________________

______________________________

______________________________

Based on what you know now, do you think the person/people you told were connected to their own higher self?

______________________________

______________________________

______________________________

Now, let us talk about those synchronicities. Knowing what you know now, what do you think the signs were telling you?

__________________________________________

__________________________________________

__________________________________________

__________________________________________

How have you used/ are using those messages in recalibrating your new life?

__________________________________________

__________________________________________

__________________________________________

__________________________________________

Can you recall how many times have you re-calibrated your life?

__________________________________________

__________________________________________

__________________________________________

__________________________________________

Have you noticed a pattern in your life events that led to the recalibration?

__________________________________________

_______________________________________

_______________________________________

_______________________________________

If you have not re-calibrated yet, what is stopping you?

_______________________________________

_______________________________________

_______________________________________

_______________________________________

If what is stopping you now was not there, what would your re-calibrated life look like? (Make a copy of this and read it every day before going to sleep so you can imagine your re-calibrated life until it becomes a reality. Then, continue doing this process until you are satisfied with the life you have created for yourself.)

_______________________________________

_______________________________________

_______________________________________

_______________________________________

### *Like the Rose of Jericho*

*The rose of Jericho is a symbol of resurrection. When you are spiritually unaligned, your heart, after many hurts, gets covered by an metaphorical outer shell to protect you, so you no longer cry or feel and become numb to what is happening to you. However, after you recalibrate, you unfold like the rose of Jericho, and you are resurrected to your new spiritual self, and then you blossom, and you stretch out into the world, touching lives. When the Rose of Jericho has no water, it is a tight ball keeping its life source on the inside, covered by a shell of protection. For some people, that shell of protection is the body fat or addiction, like an armor that they put on unknowingly so that nobody can see their true selves. It keeps them protected until they find themselves in an environment physically or mentally where their soul is nourished like the water nourishes the Rose of Jericho. After the watering, they unfurl, and the fat or addiction melts away for a beautiful soul to come out and live their highest human potential.*

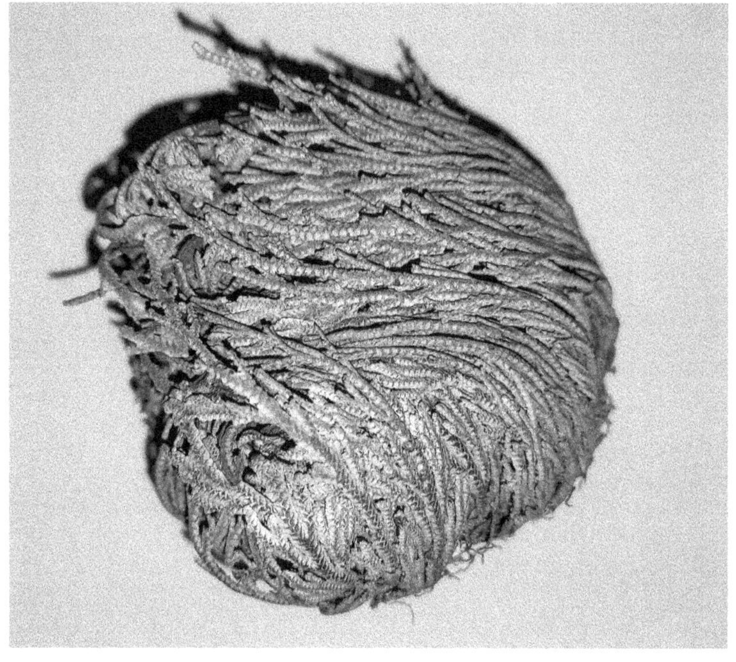

# Notes

## About the Author

Rajani is a first-generation immigrant from the Fiji Islands. She is an artist, a writer, and researcher who spends time on asking big questions about self-leadership, governing values, self-mastery, and human potential. Rajani is a doctoral candidate working on her dissertation in educational and organizational leadership and learning. During her free time, she loves to indulge in shamanic drumming, cooking, working on art, and traveling. Rajani resides in the beautiful Pacific Northwest.